First Steps through Bereavement

Why this book?

Have you, or has someone you know, suffered a bereavement?

Do you find yourself:
- Feeling isolated?
- Thinking no-one understands what you're going through?
- Worrying that you're not "normal"?
- Wondering when you'll begin to "get over it"?

Bereavement can affect you in ways you never expected and can leave you with an alarming range of emotions.

This book explains:
- The ways in which someone's death can affect you.
- How everybody grieves differently.
- How feelings of anger, guilt, or exhaustion are normal.
- Practical things you can do to look after yourself and others.

This book will help you take first steps to survive, cope, and stay healthy as you work your way through bereavement.

First Steps
through
Bereavement

Sue Mayfield

LION

A Lion Book
an imprint of
Lion Hudson plc
Wilkinson House, Jordan Hill Road,
Oxford OX2 8DR, England
www.lionhudson.com
ISBN 978 0 7459 5535 3

Distributed by:
UK: Marston Book Services, PO Box 269,
Abingdon, Oxon, OX14 4YN
USA: Trafalgar Square Publishing, 814
N. Franklin Street, Chicago, IL 60610
USA Christian Market: Kregel Publications,
PO Box 2607, Grand Rapids, MI 49501
First edition 2011
10 9 8 7 6 5 4 3 2 1 0

Acknowledgments
Poem on p. 41 taken from *Collected Poems* by Elizabeth Jennings,
published by Macmillan.

A catalogue record for this book is available
from the British Library
Typeset in 10/12 ITC Stone Serif
Printed and bound in Malta

Contents

Introduction 6

1 The first impact 13

2 Funerals and practicalities 20

3 Continuing to function 27

4 Taking your time 33

5 Expressing yourself 42

6 Talking and remembering 50

7 Staying healthy 57

8 Dealing with anger and guilt 63

9 Enjoying life again 70

10 Resurfacing 76

For the family 83

Useful resources 90

Introduction

All of us, at some point in our lives, will face bereavement. Although loss, death, and mourning are a normal, universal part of being human, for those going through it bereavement can be sheer hell.

Bereavement:

- can be isolating and lonely
- can give rise to a bewildering cocktail of emotions
- can affect you on many levels – physical, psychological, social, spiritual, and emotional
- can be difficult to talk about, even taboo.

The way we experience bereavement will be different for all of us. It's uniquely personal. There is no blueprint for how to do it and there are no rules about what is appropriate or "normal".

If you are bereaved:

- you may feel completely derailed and unable – or unwilling – to function
- you may be unable to eat, unable to make decisions, filled with remorse, consumed with rage.

But it's just as likely that:

- you will be blank and exhausted, hardly able to get out of bed in the morning, confused, or guilty that you feel no emotions whatsoever
- you may be carrying on as before, seeming to the outside eye to be "coping", behaving as if nothing has changed, and yet, in private, falling apart
- you may be wondering when it will all hit you, because so far nothing's quite sunk in and you feel completely unaltered.

However it affects you, one thing is certain: bereavement is unavoidable. There is no way round it. It may be messy, ugly, and debilitating, and well-meaning friends might seek to take your mind off the pain for a while, but unfortunately no one can do your grieving for you.

What people say

Getting through a bereavement is like riding a bucking bronco… it's all we can do to keep our fingers gripped to its mane. And just hope we don't fall off.
Virginia Ironside

So what use is a book?
Although bereavement is unavoidable, there are practical steps you can take to look after yourself while you are going through it. There are things you can

do, or avoid doing, that might cushion you a little and make life more bearable. It may be that by better understanding what you are going through, and by reading the words and stories of others who have faced losses similar to your own, you can get a handle on things and feel less alone, less isolated – less "mad" even. A book won't stop you from hurting but it might help you survive. It might also prevent you from damaging yourself and those around you by destructive patterns of behaviour or harsh words.

Who is this book for?

First Steps through Bereavement is for you if you are bereaved. In John Bunyan's story, *The Pilgrim's Progress,* the traveller has to negotiate his way across a swamp of despair known as the Slough of Despond. Marshy, waterlogged ground is a good metaphor for what bereavement can feel like, so it might be helpful to view this book as a series of stepping stones across the swampy and dangerous terrain of your grief. Although the idea of steps suggests a linear pathway – step one, step two, step three – the arrangement of chapters isn't meant to imply that you will deal with one issue and then move neatly on to the next, or indeed that you will feel as if you are progressing in any kind of measurable way. You might prefer to dip into the book at random rather than read it from cover to cover – especially if you are distracted and finding it hard to concentrate. Because bereavement can feel a bit like a rollercoaster, you may find that the book helps you some of the time and infuriates you at other times. If that's the case, I'm sorry. However you read it, my hope is that this book will help in *some* way.

- Perhaps it will keep you company so that the feeling of shared sorrow will lessen your sense of loneliness.
- Perhaps it will help you get your bearings and feel less confused.
- Perhaps it will help you feel less wobbly by reassuring you that you are completely normal.

It may give you clues about your own behaviour or other people's. Grief is very individual, but most of us function in families. Understanding the dynamics at work when families grieve together may help you navigate your way through bereavement.

This book is also for you if you are supporting someone else through a bereavement, either informally, as a friend or colleague, or more formally, as a listener or counsellor. The section *For the family* addresses you specifically, with ideas of how you can help and not make matters worse.

At a loss

We most commonly associate the word "bereavement" with the death of a relative or friend. But other losses – such as the ending of a relationship, the loss of a job, a relocation, the removal of an organ as a result of cancer, or the loss of connection with someone when they are brain-damaged, comatose, or suffering from dementia – can result in similar feelings to those experienced when someone dies. You might feel "bereaved" even if no one has died. Although this book focuses primarily on bereavement resulting from someone's death, you may find it useful if you are facing losses of other kinds.

Loss is unsettling. When someone we have a connection with isn't there any more, we feel their absence. We miss them. We miss the relationship we had with them. We miss everything they meant to us. We may be faced with significant changes as a result of what has happened, and our loss of the life-we-once-had contributes to our cumulative sense of loss. When someone we know dies, we are brought face to face with our own mortality and with the reminder that we and others we love will also die. In a culture that largely ignores the reality of death, this can leave us feeling very vulnerable.

Wherever you are, however you are feeling, and whatever the circumstances in which you find yourself reading this book, I wish you well. My hope is that *First Steps through Bereavement* will help you discover what works best for you, and that, having discovered this, you will be able to put it into practice.

Everybody goes through the same stages of grief.

Health professionals and bereavement experts have identified various stages or phases that a person may go through after a death. There are several "models" for this.

Colin Murray Parkes describes a four-stage progression:
• numbness
• pining
• disorganization
• recovery.

Elizabeth Kübler-Ross outlines a five-stage process:
• denial
• anger
• bargaining
• depression
• acceptance.

Some counsellors work with a three-stage model:
• shock
• adjustment
• reinvestment in life.

You may find that elements of your own experience correspond to one or other of these models.

But you may not go through all (or any) of these stages. And you may not necessarily go through them in any kind of logical or coherent order.

Awareness of these stages might help you by making you feel less "mad". (The phases they describe are useful waymarkers to help you make sense of your feelings.)

Or awareness of these stages might increase your anxiety. "I should be doing Depression by now and I'm still doing Anger... I thought I'd reached Recovery but I find myself Pining again..."

So, the bottom line is...

Everyone is different. If your bereavement doesn't fit any particular pattern, don't worry. It doesn't mean you're not normal. It just means you are *you*. Do it *your* way.

1

The first impact

When somebody dies, we react in many different ways. Whether we witness someone's death or are informed of it in the hours or days afterwards, our immediate response will be complex and many-layered. What was your first reaction? How did you receive the news?

Shock

If someone died suddenly and unexpectedly – in a car accident, for example, or because of an unforeseen medical incident such as a heart attack or stroke – you may have had a profound sense of shock. Perhaps you had difficulty processing the news, making sense of the reality of it. You may have experienced an absence of emotions, a feeling of being numb or "zombie-like".

If someone died after a long illness, the sense of shock may have been less intense. You may have been expecting death – waiting for it, perhaps. Doctors and nurses may have prepared you for it, describing the likely onset of the disease and the probable pattern of care, pain relief, and symptom control. If death was an end to pain or to a deterioration in life quality, there may have been an element of relief in it, a bit like finally arriving somewhere after a terrible journey. Nevertheless, the moment of death – and the finality of it – may still have come as a shock. You might have been denying the inevitability of it, hoping for some unexpected improvement – some defying of the odds, some miracle cure, maybe – and then your hopes were dashed.

Shock is often accompanied by physical symptoms such as:
- a tight chest
- shortness of breath
- difficulty swallowing
- loss of appetite
- insomnia.

Do you recognize any of these phenomena in yourself?

There's something wrong with me because I'm not upset and I don't seem to feel anything...
Feeling numb, frozen, and detached in the first days or weeks after someone's death is normal and common.

Mixed feelings

Not just the circumstances but the age of the person will have affected your first response. If someone died young, you may have a sense of injustice, of a wasted life, of missed opportunities. Your first response may have been *It's not fair!* If someone died in their nineties after a full and happy life, their death may have seemed more bearable, more natural even, and you may even have found yourself saying things like *She had a "good innings"*. On the other hand, if that person in her nineties was your great-grandmother – rock and core of your family, who had been there as a constant for your entire life – your sense of shock at her *not* being there may be quite devastating.

If a woman's husband dies in a climbing accident, she may derive some consolation from knowing that he died doing what he loved and that the risk involved in climbing was part of the thrill. But she may also be angry – *I told him not to go in those weather conditions*. There may be blame or self-blame in the mix. And what if they had had a row the day before he left and parted on bad terms, or didn't say goodbye? There may be regret, a sense of ragged edges, of unfinished business.

If someone's death is the result of suicide, the unresolved questions, the mixture of anger and dismay and betrayal and powerlessness in those left behind can be overwhelming.

"He meant the world to me..."

The impact of someone's death, in both the short and the long term, will depend on:

- whether you were close or not
- how significant they were to you
- how big a part of your life they were.

Ordinarily, the death of a spouse or child will have a greater impact than, say, the death of a cousin or an elderly aunt. But if the cousin was your childhood playmate, or lifelong rival, their death may affect you deeply. If the elderly aunt was the person you confided in when your parents' marriage was breaking apart, or the person who bailed you out when you were in debt, or your last connection to your dead parents' generation, her death might be a more significant loss than if she were a distant relation.

The person who has died may not even have been a relative or a friend. They may have been a work colleague, someone you shared an office with for twenty years, someone whose habits annoyed you on a daily basis, but who was part of the fabric of your life and whose loss leaves a hole in your existence.

The quality of the relationship will have significance too:
- whether your relationship was intimate or remote
- whether it was fractured or difficult.

For example, the death of a special friend who knew you well and had shared your highs and lows might affect you more than the death of a brother from whom you'd grown apart and rarely saw. The death of an estranged brother, however, might bring a cargo of regrets and "if onlys": *How did we come to be so distant from one another? Was it my fault? Could it have been otherwise?*

If the death was of a baby – newborn or stillborn, or miscarried in pregnancy – the pain of loss will be intensified by disappointment and by the anguish of unrealized potential, of never having had the chance to get to know this person. The bereavement may also – especially with miscarriage – be invisible. It may be unseen and unknown to others, or it may be trivialized by thoughtless comments: *You can always try for another one.*

The person who died may have been more significant to you than anyone knows. For example, if you were his secret lover or her unacknowledged gay partner, your sense of isolation might be made worse by the hidden nature of the relationship and the fact that you are excluded from the public rituals of mourning.

Questions of life and death

When someone dies, you can find yourself thinking about things you haven't really thought about before. You might be grappling with some big philosophical questions, wondering what you believe and don't believe. How you think about death will influence how you cope with it. For example, whether you see death as an abrupt ending, a terminus, an extinguishing of life – like a thread being cut or a light switched off – or whether you see it as a threshold to some other kind of life – some "life after death" – will matter. If the person's life was anguished and painful, you may see death as a resting place, a sweet sleep, a blissful silence. If you believe in God, or in heaven and hell, you might be worrying about how the person will be judged or "where" they've gone.

Not only *your* beliefs and views but those of the person who has died will have an impact:

• what *they* believed happens when you die
• whether they seemed to fight death or embraced it calmly
• whether they prepared for their death, talking about it and making plans for it and its aftermath.

Feeling that someone has had a "good death" may alleviate some of the shock and outrage that they are no longer living. Or it might make no difference whatsoever. However you rationalize a person's death and whatever you believe about what has actually happened – spiritually or biologically or theologically or existentially – the reality is the same:

- They were living; now they are dead.
- They were physically present; now they are absent.

Grasping the reality of this may take you some time. Initial responses of blankness, numbness, disbelief, and shock are common. You may even have felt euphoric, hyperactive, or more efficient than usual in the hours and days after the person's death. These reactions are part of your body's way of dealing with shock.

What people say

The body has a safety mechanism [numbness] that protects us from the tidal wave of emotion that might otherwise push our heart rate and blood pressure up to a physically dangerous level.
Dr Tony Lake

Mythbuster

The fact that I feel unemotional at the moment means this person's death hasn't affected me and I'm fine...
Your feelings of detachment may be part of a normal shock reaction, cushioning you in the early days of bereavement. You may find that you become *more* (not less) emotional as this shock begins to wear off.

2

Funerals and practicalities

Dealing with the funeral is the first task most bereaved people face. If you are responsible for organizing the ceremony, this can be a mixed bag. Some bereaved people welcome the focus that the planning and practicalities give to the first days after someone's death. Others see the funeral as a necessary hurdle to be got over before the proper business of bereavement can begin.

What people say

The day you bury him is a day of chores and crowds, of hands false and true to be shaken, of the immediate cares of mourning. The dead will not really die until tomorrow, when silence is round you again.
Antoine de Saint-Exupéry

Making decisions

There are many decisions to be made at a time when you may feel unfit to make decisions at all. Will the person be buried or cremated? If buried, then where? Will it be a churchyard burial, a municipal cemetery, or a woodland plot? If cremated, then what will be done with the ashes? Will the funeral be led by a minister or faith leader, or will you opt for a humanist ceremony? And what will the service amount to? Will you have readings or eulogies or music or prayers? Who will say what, and how will you decide whom to involve and what to include? What sort of scale will it be on – will it be lavish or simple? And what will be its tone?

As with so many aspects of bereavement, there is no blueprint – no right or wrong way of doing it – and, increasingly, families tailor their ceremonies to fit their own wishes, beliefs, and tastes. But such a range of choices can be bewildering.

If you are involved in planning a funeral, the following questions may be useful in guiding your decisions.

What is a funeral for?

Is it primarily a celebration of the person's life – a chance to remember them and give thanks? Or is it principally an opportunity to grieve and acknowledge your sadness and dismay? (Because it's usually both, it is increasingly common to have two events – a burial or cremation and then a thanksgiving or memorial service. Some people have both services on the same day. Others leave a gap of weeks or months between the two events.)

Who is the funeral for?

Is it for the person who has died, or is it for the grieving friends and relatives who are left behind? Should the focus be on commending the dead person to the afterlife (if you believe in an afterlife), on saying goodbye, or on consoling the bereaved in their loss? Who is likely to be there, and how are they likely to be feeling?

What were the wishes of the person who has died?

Did they leave instructions about the sort of funeral they wanted? Did they express strong opinions about other people's funerals they had attended? What would be most appropriate in the circumstances? What would best reflect the character and outlook of the person?

Carrying out someone's wishes with regard to their funeral plans might feel like a final act of tenderness, but it is important to think about your own needs too and about the implications of decisions that you make immediately after someone's death. For example, if he is buried, will you be able to visit the grave afterwards? Or if she is cremated, will you want to bury her ashes somewhere or scatter them in a favourite spot? For some, going to a specific place to be quiet or sad or simply to remember the person who has died can be helpful in the first months and years after death. For others, it will be an irrelevance. If you are recently bereaved, it may be difficult to know how you will feel in two or five or ten years' time and what will have been most helpful for you, so try not to be rushed into decisions you can't undo.

Help!

There is good practical advice about funeral options and arrangements, including comparative costs, on the websites **www.ifishoulddie.co.uk** and **www.dying.about.com** (follow the link "Grief and Mourning: What's Normal?" to the article "How to Plan a Funeral or Memorial Service").

The book *We Need to Talk About the Funeral: 101 Practical Ways to Commemorate and Celebrate a Life* by Jane Morrell and Simon Smith is a very useful compendium of ideas and information.

Funerals can be very expensive. The website **www.patient.co.uk** has an excellent section on "Benefits for Bereaved People" (follow the link from "Benefits & Finance") and the New Zealand Government website **http://newzealand.govt.nz** has some very good factsheets on bereavement and wills (simply type "bereavement and wills" into the search bar).

Physical contact

Before you even reach the day of the funeral you will make decisions about the person's body. If you weren't there when the person died, do you want to see the body? Do you want your children to see it? People have strong feelings about this. Some might say, "I don't want to see him. I prefer to remember him alive." Others might say, "I need to see her body in order to grasp the reality of her death – so that I can't kid myself that she hasn't really died."

If it is your child or your partner – someone with whose body you are very familiar and where touch has been an important part of your relationship in life – you may want to touch and hold the person's body after they die. In Western society we tend to delegate the responsibility of dealing with a dead person's body to undertakers, who will often remove it with great haste, and as a result we are unfamiliar with death and are perhaps squeamish about it. But in other parts of the world it is normal practice for families to prepare the dead for their funerals within the family home – to wash and dress them, comb hair, trim beards, and adorn with jewellery. How you feel about a person's body after death will be influenced by your culture and beliefs. Do you see the body as an empty shell, a "tattered overcoat", so that the essence of the person – their soul or spirit – is now free to exist somewhere else? Or is the body something to be honoured and cherished? Is it your last point of contact with a loved one's physical presence? You may want to savour the texture of their skin and hair, their smell, their shape, for as long as you possibly can. Only you know what feels appropriate and what you are comfortable with, so try not to be too constrained by what other people think. Do or don't do what is most helpful to you.

It may be that seeing or touching the person's body isn't an option for you.

Perhaps you are too far away. Perhaps the person has died in a natural disaster, a terrorist attack, or in armed conflict, and their body was never retrieved or identified. Perhaps you miscarried a baby in early pregnancy.

How do you mark someone's death when there is no body to bury? You might consider having some other sort of ceremony to give a focal point to your grief. You could:
- plant a tree
- build a cairn of stones
- write memories and thoughts on paper, then burn it and bury or scatter the ashes.

Public grief

If you haven't been involved in planning someone's funeral, it might be that arriving at the funeral and seeing their coffin is the moment when you really grasp the news that they are dead.

Funerals are very public events. There may be people there you haven't seen for a long time or people you've never met. If you are the dead person's spouse or son or daughter or parent, you may find yourself being the centre of attention, being greeted or hugged by crying strangers. People may tell you stories or express sentiments about the person who has died. Their words might feel a bit overwhelming, but sometimes anecdotes and good wishes at the funeral – along with those expressed in letters and cards of condolence – can be a great source of comfort in the bleak days following the ceremony.

Dealing with other people's emotions as well as your own can be tough, though. Depending on how comfortable you are with showing your feelings, you may want to be left alone to weep, or you may prefer to hold it together and keep your composure. You may be aware of children or parents for whom you want to be strong. You may be terrified that if you express any emotions, you will be overwhelmed by the ferocity of your feelings and will completely go to pieces. Or you might be feeling so numb that you sail through the day in a blur, simply doing what is necessary.

Mythbuster

Public displays of emotion at funerals are self-indulgent and embarrass others.

It's OK to be emotional at funerals. Most people will be expecting you to be upset. Perhaps by crying you will give *them* permission to cry. But it's fine to be private too. Try to be yourself and do what feels natural. Try not to worry about what other people think.

3

Continuing to function

Most of us are unsettled by change. Bereavement involves major changes – you are adjusting to the reality that someone significant isn't there any more – so you may feel as if you want to cling to every vestige of familiarity. You might want – as far as you are able – to hold on to the rhythms and routines that you had before the person died. Going to work, taking the children to school, walking the dog, and keeping up with hobbies and sports may be part of your coping strategies. Continued patterns function like scaffolding poles to stop you falling apart.

But beware. Being over-busy and driving yourself too hard can be a trap that may leave you feeling worse further down the line.

So how do you know when activity has become over-activity? How do you tell the difference between being healthily occupied and unhealthily distracted?

When should I go back to work?

Going back to work immediately after someone has died may be a financial necessity. But, if you have some choice and flexibility, think about what is best for you.

What people say

I went back to work straight away. I needed the safety net of routine and company.
A medical receptionist

I went back to work too quickly and couldn't cope with emotional situations. About a year later I crashed completely and had to go on antidepressants.
A nurse

Work allowed me to switch off from things at home, but my concentration was poor and I found making decisions difficult.
An IT project manager

Ask yourself:
- Can I do my job safely and competently?
- Am I sufficiently robust to cope with difficulties and setbacks?

 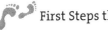

• Would a gradual or delayed return to work be more beneficial in the long term?

Keeping going

Getting out of bed in the morning, doing housework, digging the garden, going to clubs you went to before, taking exercise, or volunteering might have some therapeutic value. You may even be motivated by a sense that the person who has died would want you to keep functioning. *He wouldn't want me to mope and be miserable… She'd want me to finish building the patio we planned together… I mustn't neglect his geraniums!* You might find yourself taking on roles that were formerly the responsibility of the person who has died, or championing their causes.

If you have people or animals who are dependent on you, you might simply have to get on with caring for them. For children going through bereavement, keeping some semblance of normality is vital. They are already dealing with the loss of someone they love, so the more you can maintain normal activities such as swimming or football practice or friends' birthday parties, the better things will be. Continuity will help bereaved children feel safe in a frightening and unpredictable world.

In and out of grief

Recent research by psychologists Stroebe and Schut identifies the *Dual Process Model*. They describe bereaved people oscillating between expressing their feelings and controlling their feelings, focusing alternately on loss and on the restoration of normality. Stroebe and Schut's work suggests that dipping in and out of grief is normal and healthy, and that becoming absorbed in tasks or activities that give temporary respite from the reality of loss is a useful coping mechanism.

What's the point?

But what if keeping going feels pointless? What if daily chores and concerns feel absurd or even obscene in the light of the fact that your husband or daughter or best friend has just died? You might actually feel that shopping or cooking or watching TV is disloyal to the person who has died. *How dare I do these things when she can't? How can I trivialize his death by carrying on with the superficial stuff of daily life?* You might find that you have no appetite for the things you used to do before, or that they are tainted by what C. S. Lewis described as the "shabby flatness" of life viewed through the lens of a bereavement. But however ridiculous continuing to function might feel, it would seem that, on balance, it will help you in the long term. Research suggests that this is true for both men and women, though in general men are more inclined to throw themselves into busyness after a significant death than women are.

Filling the void

If you've been caring for someone who's been ill for a long time, it could be that their death brings an end to many aspects of your previous routine. Perhaps you've been fitting in regular hospital visits, dealing with calls from a Macmillan nurse, doing someone's laundry, or going without sleep to sit with someone at night. Their death has left a big hole in your life, and maybe you feel as if any sense of structure has crumbled. You might now want to pack your life with new activities in order to fill the void. Try to avoid this temptation. Joining new clubs or taking up new hobbies or interests may be a good idea in time, but try to be honest with yourself about why you are doing them.

• Are new activities primarily a distraction from the reality of bereavement?
• Am I simply avoiding loneliness or an empty house or a sense of absence by keeping busy?
• Am I ready to take on new responsibilities and commitments, or might I end up feeling overwhelmed and exhausted?

Mythbuster

Keeping busy is the best way to cope with bereavement.

It might be that your busyness is a smokescreen and that by rushing around doing things you are avoiding the reality of your loss. This sort of distraction has been likened to pressing "pause" on a video or DVD. Activities may give you a break from your sadness or loneliness, but when you return, the "tape" will not have advanced and you will be exactly where you were when you last pressed "pause".

Try to give yourself time and permission to grieve, and don't leave yourself with no opportunity to think.

Chaos!
Routines can help create a sense of order in chaos, but you may feel incapable of functioning from day to day. It is common for people experiencing bereavement to be disorganized, forgetful, and chaotic, so don't be alarmed if you feel less efficient than usual or if life seems to be a bit rough round the edges. If people offer to help you by collecting your children from school, walking your dog, or doing your shopping, then let them. Usually, the more time elapses after a bereavement, the more the offers of practical help dry up, so swallow your pride and let your friends and neighbours help you now.

And remember...
Avoid making major decisions or drastic changes to your lifestyle in the first weeks or months after a significant death.

Give yourself time to feel your way into your "new" life and don't rush.

4

Taking your time

I said in the last chapter that you should take your time and try not to rush. But how long should bereavement last? How long does grieving take? What's acceptable? What's normal? What sort of time frame should you have in mind? Six months? A year? Two years? Five years?

What are the rules?

A hundred years ago there were much clearer rules about mourning, or at least about the outward observance of a bereavement. A widow would wear black clothing – "widow's weeds" – for two years after her husband's death; parents of dead children or children of dead parents wore black for one year; bereaved siblings wore black for six months.

Nowadays, these customs – and other practices such as doffing caps, drawing curtains, and lowering flags – have all but disappeared.

Other cultures mark the passing of time after a death more formally. In the Jewish tradition, special prayers are recited every day for a year and a candle is burned at sundown every evening until the first anniversary of a death. Greek Orthodox Christians say prayers at three, nine, and forty days and then three, six, and twelve months after a death, then annually thereafter. Some cultures mark the "end" of mourning. In rural Greece a body is buried in a temporary marble grave for five years, after which it is exhumed and the bones placed in a communal village grave. The "clean" bones are taken as a sign that the person's soul is now purified and living in paradise.

"Getting over it"

So where does that leave us in modern society, where an employer may grant just a few days' compassionate leave and where friends and work colleagues may be expecting you to be back to normal in a matter of weeks? People often talk about "getting over it", as though the death of someone we loved were a dose of the flu!

What people say

... the world rushes on and doesn't have the patience or the time to be tolerant for too long with us and our loss,

Readjusting might be a better way to think of bereavement than *getting over it*. Loss and grief aren't diseases from which you will eventually recover. Rather, bereavement is a process of readjusting to life without the person you have lost and affirming the new and continuing relationship you have in death. How long that process takes will be as individual as everything else about bereavement.

The "10-Mile Mourning Bridge"

Writers Ruth Huber and Judy Bryant, working with bereaved people in a hospice in the USA, have devised the 10-Mile Mourning Bridge, a linear scale where 0 is the point prior to grieving and 10 is the point at which grieving is no longer the primary focus of life. The purpose of this visual analogue is to provide some means to self-assess "progress" through the process of bereavement.

Many of us like the idea of being able to measure our progress, to get some perspective on how we're doing in relation to others or "the norm", but the pattern of our journey through bereavement may not be neat or predictable. It's highly likely that after the initial sense of shock and numbness starts to recede you will begin to feel worse, not better. Maybe offers of help and support are more scarce than they were at the start. Maybe you feel less cushioned than you did, and now your sense of aching loneliness just hurts, as though an anaesthetic were wearing off. You might be tired and irritable, more raw, less able to cope now that the rush of adrenaline that saw you through the first days and weeks has faded. Perhaps you feel under pressure to cope or to appear to be coping. Or maybe you just feel weary with the length of time it all seems to be taking and with the sense that for every step forward, you seem to take another step (or even two steps) backwards. It may help to know that others have experienced this sense of going round in circles. Here is what C. S. Lewis wrote in his book *A Grief Observed*, which describes what life was like for him after his wife died: "Grief is like a long valley, a winding valley where any bend may reveal a totally new landscape... Sometimes... you are presented with exactly the same sort of country you thought you had left behind miles ago. That is when you wonder whether the valley isn't a circular trench."

Mythbuster

You will feel better the more time elapses after someone's death.
Overall, in the bigger long-term picture, it's likely that the intensity of feelings you are experiencing will gradually lessen and that your bereavement won't dominate life as much as it does now.

But it's not uncommon to feel *worse* six months or a year or even two years after a significant death. Don't be alarmed if you feel worse before you feel better.

You are adapting to the reality of your loss and your body's protection strategies aren't functioning as well as they did at the start. It's as if, little by little, you're being deprived of the things people describe in the early days as "cushions", "cotton wool in the ears", "bubble wrap", "a sense that nothing is real", so that you can see and hear and feel things more starkly.

Sorting out the stuff

So when is the best time to sort out a person's belongings, to get rid of clothes and shoes, dispose of personal items, move and marshall all the bits of stuff that we accumulate in our lifetime? Should we do it straight away or is it all right to wait?

Sometimes the pace is forced by a house being sold or a property vacated, so decisions – what to throw away, what to keep, who gets what, what's of significance and what isn't – have to made quickly. But if there's no rush, when do you do it, and is it OK if you leave it a while?

I knew a man once whose neighbour thought she was being helpful by stripping his house of every last trace of his wife's presence on the day after her death. Clothes, hairbrushes, slippers, face creams were all bundled into bin bags and whisked away while he was out of the house.

Sometimes people assume that if you've still got your dead wife's toothbrush in the bathroom mug, then you won't be able to "move on". Or if you've left your dad's gardening boots by the back door, you haven't really accepted he's dead. Or if you can't bear to give away your son's skateboard or change the sheets that still smell of him, then you're somehow "stuck" in your grief.

Only *you* can judge when is the right time to tackle these practical matters. If you think it would help you to take everything to a charity shop straight away, then do it. If you would prefer to wait a few months or even a few years, then try not to bow to pressure from others, who might not know what's best for you. If you're dreading sorting things and putting it off because you can't face the enormity of the task, ask a friend or relative to help you. Sort as much as you can bear and then leave the rest for another day.

Don't underestimate how much comfort you might get from items which remind you of the person who has died, particularly things which carry their scent. I knew a widower who kept his wife's nightdress under his pillow for more than a year after she died. Comfort objects such as shirts or scarves are especially important for children, so try to be sensitive to what will help other members of your family if a child's parent or sibling has died.

You might like to pass things on to people who will treasure them or use them, or to give them to charity shops so that they can be recycled.

Ask yourself:

- What can I face doing?
- What will help me and my family most?
- What are my motives for keeping or shedding these belongings? For example, am I keeping my wife's clothes in the wardrobe because the colours and fabrics remind me of her and are a comfort, or am I keeping them because I haven't really accepted that she isn't coming back? Am I fooling myself that she is away on holiday, or that this is a bad dream from which I will finally awake?

Be kind to yourself, but be honest too.

It may take a long time to fully grasp the harsh reality that someone's death is permanent and irreversible, and you may find you accept this piece by piece rather than all at once, so pace yourself and go at a speed that suits you.

And what about the ashes?

If a person has been cremated and you've retained the ashes, you will have another tricky decision to make at some point. Where will you put the ashes, and when is the right time to do it? *Shall we scatter them in that wood she loved at bluebell time? Shall we plant a tree on the first anniversary of his death and bury them there? Shall we wait a while and then inter them in a cemetery or garden of remembrance?*

Sometimes people are reluctant to part with ashes, feeling that they are the last trace of physical contact they have with the person who has died. Other people feel unsentimental and get rid of them as soon as they can. Do what you think is best, and try to discuss your feelings and thought processes with other people who might feel strongly about the decision.

The first year

Many bereaved people say that the first year is the worst. Getting past the person's birthday, the first Christmas or Mother's Day without them, and reaching the anniversary of their death are all major landmarks. Once a whole year has gone by you might be less conscious of the passage of time. *This time last year he was… It's a year since she was diagnosed…*

Psychologists concur that disruptions to a person's normal functioning, and phenomena such as dysphoria (pathological sadness and low mood – the opposite of "euphoria"), are usually the most extreme in the first year of a bereavement. This isn't always the case, however. Some people find the second or third year worse than the first. Everybody is different.

Remember, if you start to feel worse rather than better, that doesn't mean you are failing or that you are doing something wrong.

Time is a great healer.

This cliché is often trotted out where bereavement is concerned. It may, in broad terms, be true, but the nitty-gritty of experience may be more messy and painful.

The English poet Elizabeth Jennings wrote:

Time does not heal.
It makes a half-stitched scar
That can be broken and you feel
Grief as total as in its first hour.

5

Expressing yourself

Grieving can give rise to complex and powerful emotions. You might feel terrible sadness, loneliness, emptiness, rage, or regret. You might find yourself experiencing several conflicting emotions all at once or lurching from one emotional state to another, so that you feel as though you're being flung about in a violent storm.

So how do you deal with these emotions and how can you best express them? You might be bottling up emotions for fear of embarrassing yourself or others. You might be putting on a brave face, struggling to cope, telling others you are fine. This composed exterior might be your armour – your way of shielding yourself from the possibility of meltdown in the face of emotions that are more intense than you could have imagined. Maybe the thought of expressing emotions fills you with terror. *What if I am overwhelmed by my feelings? What if they flood over me like a tidal wave?*

For many of us, showing emotions – especially negative emotions – goes against our upbringing and culture. We worry that we might be a nuisance or that people will think less of us if we seem not to be holding ourselves together.

Mythbuster

Keeping a lid on my emotions is better for everyone.
Acknowledging and expressing your emotions might do you *more* good. Denying feelings, or suppressing them because you think they are unacceptable, might make you more likely to suffer from depression or stress-related illnesses in the long term.

Tears or not?
In some cultures, tears are seen as a sign of weakness. For example, in Rwanda – a country that has experienced harrowing suffering in recent decades – *not* crying is considered a badge of courage for both sexes. In some religions, crying is seen as defying God – *If this person's death is God's will, I shouldn't oppose it with my tears.* Older people raised in a "stiff upper lip" British culture may, in childhood, have been schooled not to cry.

What about you?

How do you feel about tears? Are you someone who cries easily? Do you find yourself apologizing if you burst into tears in front of someone else? Do you consider tears self-indulgent and think that, by weeping, you are just wallowing in grief?

What people say

I felt I had a bottomless well of tears.
Joan, when her daughter died

He would go outside with the lawnmower and wail privately at the end of the garden.
Penny, describing her husband's response to their child's death

I cry a lot. I find it makes me feel better. It's no good bottling it up.
Carol, after the death of her husband

Often, crying can bring a sense of release, like letting something out. It can feel cleansing or cathartic. But tears can also be exhausting and debilitating.

What if you want to cry but can't? The tears won't come. You feel as if your emotions are too big for tears or that you are "all cried out". Try not to berate yourself for how you feel or don't feel. Try not to worry too much about what others think or expect.

Cry if it helps you. If you find yourself welling up with tears at inconvenient moments, be kind to yourself and try not to apologize. Carry tissues. Wear waterproof mascara. Trust your friends or colleagues to take it in their stride. Or lock the door and cry in private where no one else will be upset.

Why do I feel like this?

As well as sadness you might be feeling:

- a sense of desolation or despair
- restless and unable to settle
- a sense of loss that feels like a physical ache – as if you've been "disembowelled", "hollowed out", or "stripped bare"
- unbearably lonely – yearning for the person who has died
- hopeless, or even suicidal.

It's very likely that the more you have loved someone, the more their death will hurt; the greater your sense of connectedness with them in life, the more abject your sense of separation now. As C. S. Lewis said, "The pain now is part of the happiness then. That's the deal." You might also be feeling angry or guilty, but we'll look more closely at these feelings in Chapter 8.

What about the people around me?

Most of us belong to families of some sort. When *we* are bereaved, other people will be bereaved too. But your son or wife or mother might grieve differently from you. For example, you may have lost your wife and feel desperate and heartbroken, but your son who has lost his mother may be grumpy and blaming. You may be trying to control your own feelings in order to help him with his. The way you manage your feelings may cause you to clash.

If your husband is responding to the death of your baby by being practical and unemotional, and you want to sit and howl, the contrast in the way you are behaving may increase your sense of isolation. Lack of common ground and understanding in bereavement can do great damage to a relationship. Cruse Bereavement Care report that over 90 per cent of couples facing the death of a child separate within two years.

People who let you be yourself and grieve in your own way are worth their weight in gold, as are friends who will allow you to express feelings without trying to distract you or change the subject. As one bereaved woman said, "People who risked my tears – and their own – were best of all."

"Better out than in"

The mother of a childhood friend used to say of vomiting, "Better out than in." If you believe that the same is true of strong feelings, then how can you express them? And how can you do this constructively rather than destructively?

- *Be honest.* Try to get in touch with what you are really feeling. Be aware of your emotions and their complexity.

- *Take yourself seriously.* Give yourself permission to feel what you are feeling. Don't trivialize or rationalize your emotions. You are bereaved – you don't have to be reasonable!

- *Find somewhere safe.* Go for a walk by yourself or shut the door and pull the curtains. If you want company, find someone who will be robust and non-judgmental and will listen without flinching. If there is no one in your circle of family or friends whom you would risk being upset in front of, consider seeing a counsellor. (You'll find a list of organizations offering counselling in the *Useful resources* section at the back of the book.)

- *Write.* If you find it difficult to express feelings, writing may help. You could write lists of words or feelings, keep a journal, write poems, or even try writing letters to the person who has died. Afterwards it might be therapeutic to burn or shred what you have written.

• *Set yourself limits.* If you fear that venting your feelings will be like opening floodgates, it may be helpful to set yourself parameters. Decide, for example, that you will cry or shout or write for, say, an hour and then arrange for a friend to pop in or go for a walk or watch a television programme. Recognize that emotions are exhausting and let yourself rest and switch off too.

Not in front of the children...

Children, especially, need to jump in and out of feelings when they are bereaved. A child may be crying and sad one moment and then happily playing the next. Try to give children opportunities to express emotions in appropriate and natural ways, and don't feel that they need to be distracted to keep them from becoming upset. You may feel that if you express *your* feelings you will alarm your children, but it could be that by crying with them and in front of them you give them permission to show *their* feelings too.

Children may find drawing or making things useful in expressing their grief. Making masks or icing cakes or cookies with happy, sad, angry, or frightened faces can be a way of helping children talk about their feelings.

However your family functions, try to give each other space to be sad and don't assume that *your* way of expressing stuff is the right or only way to do it.

But what if I feel nothing?

All this talk of emotions may be causing you to think there is something wrong with you. Maybe you feel utterly blank. You're not sad or angry or bewildered or lost. In fact, you feel nothing at all. Just dead inside. Perhaps you wish you were *more* upset. Perhaps you feel guilty that you don't feel any of the emotions I've listed. (I'll come back to guilt in Chapter 8.) For now, try not to worry.

However...

- If you're avoiding situations that might make you upset, you could try to do this less.
- If you've put off visiting the place where he died or some spot that was special to you both, perhaps going there will help you get in touch with some feelings.
- If you've avoided going through her things, listening to her favourite music, reading the letters people sent you after she died, maybe now is the time to risk doing that.

You are the person who knows you best, so try to treat yourself as a patient friend would treat you, and cut yourself some slack.

6

Talking and remembering

Some people find talking about things easier than others. If you're a natural talker, you may find you want to talk about the person who has died and about the way their death has left you feeling. You may want to tell stories about them, go over the details of their death, or describe their last days and hours. If you are lucky, you will have friends who will listen and let you talk.

You may find, however, that other people try to silence you or change the subject to "take your mind off it". Worse still, people might avoid you altogether for fear of not knowing what to say to you or of saying something embarrassing or inappropriate. It's common for bereaved people to feel isolated because other people don't know how to behave and are terrified of getting it wrong.

Novelist Alice Jolly, writing in *The Guardian* newspaper about the death of her baby daughter, said:

Less than a month after her death it was our son's third birthday and my husband and I organized a party for him. About thirty adults attended… accompanying their children. But with the exception of two close friends, no one mentioned Laura's death. The shock of that silence was nearly as bad as the shock of my daughter's death.

Wanting to talk, and feeling that other people won't let you, can leave you feeling frustrated and alone.

If, however, you find articulating difficult, you might be avoiding talking about your bereavement altogether. Perhaps you are reluctant to start conversations in case you upset yourself or others. You may be thinking that talking won't help – that it will only make you more sad, more lonely.

It's good to talk…

Some cultures recognize the value of talking after a death by ritualizing the act of shared talking. For example, in the Jewish tradition, close family will "sit shiva" for a week after a burial – sitting in their living room while friends, relatives, and neighbours visit with food and tell stories of the person who has died.

This custom gives a community permission to laugh, cry, and share memories together.

In Muslim societies, too, family and friends visit the bereaved to pass on condolences and swap stories, taking off their shoes when entering the house and covering their heads when speaking of the person who has died.

Families

When a whole family is going through bereavement, there may be those who want to talk and those who don't. This mismatch may cause tensions and misunderstandings. For example, one bereaved sibling may want to talk about his dead mother all the time, whereas his sister never mentions her; one grieving grandparent may long to talk about her dead grandchild, whereas her husband responds with silence. If it is too difficult to talk to the people closest to you, it may help to talk to a neutral stranger. Outside agencies such as Cruse Bereavement Care, which offer counselling services, can give you space to talk without fear of causing hurt or offence.

Keeping the memories alive

Remembering the dead is an important part of bereavement. You are adjusting to living *without* someone, but you are also acknowledging and honouring what they meant to you and the unique place they have in your life.

What do you remember most about the person who has died?

Maybe you fear that, as time goes by, you will forget them. Children, in particular, often fear they won't be able to remember someone who has died. Activities which help children talk together and cherish their memories, such as creating memory boxes, Christmas tree baubles, and special books, can make a significant difference to them in the years that follow a bereavement.

Talking about a dead parent or sibling may be especially important at times of growth and change. For example, a boy whose father died when he was five may have a renewed desire to talk about him when he is fifteen and going through adolescence, or twenty-five and making important choices.

What was Dad doing when he was my age? What would he think about this? Or say about that?

Write it down

Writing memories down can help. A friend of mine, when she knew she was terminally ill, wrote letters to each of her children telling them things she thought they'd like to know when they grew up. Writing can be a way of capturing things so they won't be lost.

Another friend recalled asking friends and relatives to write down all the things they had said about her son at his funeral because she knew she wouldn't remember afterwards and she wanted to be able to revisit all their anecdotes and tributes.

"Don't speak ill of the dead!"

When someone dies, it's quite likely you'll have bad memories as well as good. Maybe their death was traumatic and things happened which confused or frightened you. Maybe they were ill and the medication they were on made them behave uncharacteristically – they said or did things that you keep remembering. Maybe your relationship with them was just plain complicated. Some bereavement counsellors give their clients "holding objects" such as pebbles to enable them to speak about mixed feelings. A smooth pebble might represent the memories that are comfortable and ordinary; a rough stone, memories that are painful; a shiny or colourful pebble, memories that are very precious. Just as all three pebbles can be held in your hand at once, so you might be carrying a tangle of memories – good, bad, and indifferent.

It's tempting when someone dies only to mention the good things. Often we have a tendency to "sanctify" people who've died so that they become more and more perfect and less and less like their real selves as the years go by.

Talking can help you to:

• remember accurately
• understand things that have confused you
• "get your story straight".

Talking too much about someone who has died is unhealthy – it's "brooding".

Talk as much as you want to. It's a normal, healthy part of grief. Talking about a person who has died helps you acknowledge their ongoing *presence* while simultaneously adjusting to their *absence*.

What about talking *to* the dead?

If it's normal to talk about the dead, is it also normal to talk *to* them? *Am I crazy to keep talking to her photograph? Is there something wrong with me for walking round an empty house chatting to him? Is it OK to ask her things, or tell her what I'm thinking?*

Conversations with people who have recently died are remarkably common. Death may be an abrupt ending to someone's life, but a relationship that has existed for years doesn't automatically stop when someone dies. You still feel connected to them. You still care what they think or might have thought. Talking to someone who has died is very natural. It doesn't mean you're going mad. It doesn't mean you've suddenly become a spiritualist. It doesn't even necessarily mean you believe they can hear you. But it's part of your processing of all that has happened and part of getting to grips with what the consequences of your bereavement are going to feel like.

You may find as time passes that you speak to the person less or that conversations become more internalized.

What about God?

If you have faith, it may help you to talk to God about your bereavement. Try to be honest in your prayers. If you are feeling angry or confused or hostile towards God, try to articulate this. There's an ancient tradition of crying out to God in bewilderment and sadness in the books of Psalms and Lamentations in the Jewish Scriptures. You might find that reading them helps you say what you want to say.

7

Staying healthy

This chapter is about looking after yourself in the months following someone's death. Bereavement can disrupt your normal patterns of eating, sleeping, and functioning, so the more you take care of your health, the better.

Sleep and dreams

You may be having difficulty sleeping. Perhaps you find it difficult to get to sleep – you can't switch off the thoughts going round and round in your head. Perhaps you're sleeping fitfully or you're having vivid dreams. You dream that the person who has died is still alive after all and then you wake up and remember they're not. Or you're having nightmares filled with disturbing disasters and death.

Maybe, if your partner has died, you're avoiding going to bed in the first place. You can't bear to get into an empty bed. You miss the closeness and intimacy too much.

You might be feeling exhausted – incredibly and profoundly tired. Fatigue and poor concentration are common, especially in the first year of bereavement.

But you might also have the opposite problem. Perhaps you're feeling euphoric or hyperactive – living with a heightened sense of reality as though the volume button is turned up too loud, as though you can't slow down and stop.

What people say

After he died I wanted to sleep to oblivion. It was a monumental effort to get out of bed in the morning.
Louise, after her husband's death

I felt as if I didn't need much sleep and often worked late into the night, seeking the numbing effects of busyness.
Nick, after the death of his wife

It is so exhausting, this feeling of lethargic misery…
Rebecca Abrams, in her book *When Parents Die*

Exercise
Taking regular exercise and getting out into the fresh air might help you feel better and even sleep better. Activities that are gentle, rhythmic, and repetitive, such

as swimming, walking, or yoga, can be very therapeutic. Do them, even if you don't feel like it.

If, however, you are normally a fit and sporty person, a vigorous workout at the gym or a gruelling game of squash may help you feel "unclenched" and better able to relax.

Listening to music, taking a warm bath, or watching some escapist TV before you go to bed might help you get to sleep more easily. If you're someone who finds writing helpful, keep a notebook by your bed and, when you wake in the night, write until you feel tired again.

Eating properly

You may have found that your eating patterns are all over the place.

- You've got no appetite – food doesn't interest you.
- You're so distracted you forget to eat regular meals.
- You've got no energy and can't be bothered to cook.
- There's nothing in the fridge and you can't face shopping.
- You comfort eat – craving biscuits, chocolate, or fast food.

Sudden weight loss, or weight gain, often occurs during bereavement. Maybe you can't see the point in eating. If your partner has died and you're cooking for one instead of two, perhaps it feels meaningless. Or maybe your partner was the one who cooked, and you feel lost and helpless in the kitchen.

However you're feeling about food, remember that *you matter*. Eating regularly and well is important and will enable you to stay healthy so that you can face life with as much physical strength as possible.

If friends or neighbours offer to cook, leave food on your doorstep, or invite you out for meals, try to accept their help. Often if people don't know how to help you, feeding you is the first thing they'll think of. They'll guess that eating may be low on your list of priorities and they'll probably be right. Some cultures formalize this practical support. For example, the Muslim tradition requires mourners *not* to cook for themselves for forty days after a death, during which time relatives and neighbours supply food.

If no one offers to feed you and you can't face feeding yourself, take vitamin supplements to boost your well-being and strengthen your immune system.

Drinking

If you're feeling overwhelmingly miserable, have lost all sense of purpose, and can't sleep, it can be easy to drink more than you normally do. It might be tempting to dull the pain or lift your mood artificially by having a drink, but try not to increase your consumption of alcohol, especially if you are spending a lot of time on your own. If you are worried that you are drinking too much, tell someone – a trusted friend or your doctor.

My own health seems insignificant. What does it matter, when the person I loved has died?
Bereavement often brings a sense of futility and a loss of purpose. Even if, at this moment, you feel as if nothing matters and what you do and don't do is unimportant, remember that *you matter*! Look after yourself. Nurture yourself.

Stress-related illnesses
Doctors report that it is very common for bereaved people to visit them more frequently than usual, especially in the first year after a death. As well as feeling tired or unable to sleep, you may be experiencing any number of stress-related symptoms:
- aches and pains
- eczema or itchy skin
- nausea
- difficulty swallowing
- palpitations
- digestive difficulties, colitis, or irritable bowel syndrome (IBS).

There is evidence that grief and bereavement can affect a person's immune system, making them more susceptible to illness – more likely to become "run down".

Be kind to yourself. Try to listen to your body and know what you need.

- If you're doing too much, slow down.
- If you need to go to bed and rest, try to arrange for this to happen.
- If you need a slap-up meal or a bracing walk up a mountain, make this a priority.

"I think I'm depressed..."

Feeling sad, low, demotivated, despairing – even suicidal – is normal in bereavement. It doesn't mean you are ill or need antidepressants.

However, *some* people who are bereaved – some psychologists say 5–10 per cent – may become depressed and need help. This is more likely to happen if you have what are sometimes referred to as "traumatic" or "complicated" grief symptoms – for example:

- the death was unusually shocking or violent;
- the dynamics of your family are particularly conflicted and difficult;
- you have a predisposition towards depressive illness;
- you have experienced multiple, cumulative losses.

If you are worried that you might be depressed, ask for help: either talk to your doctor, or consider counselling or CBT (cognitive behaviour therapy).

Above all, take your health – physical, mental, and emotional – seriously. You owe it to yourself and to the person who has died.

8

Dealing with anger and guilt

Most people expect to feel sad when someone dies, but maybe they *don't* expect to feel angry. Anger, however, is a very normal part of bereavement – so much so that journalist Virginia Ironside subtitled her book *You'll Get Over It* "The Rage of Bereavement". If you are feeling angry, furious, enraged, or just plain irritable, then you are not alone.

Why am I angry?
Maybe you are angry because you feel the person shouldn't have died. Their death was preventable or it was the fault of someone's neglect or incompetence.

He was having routine surgery and there were unexpected complications. She was involved in an accident that someone else caused. If his symptoms had been investigated sooner, he might have lived longer or not died at all.

In your anger you may be blaming someone or something. This blame might, of course, be entirely justified, especially if somebody has died as the result of someone else's actions or even malice. In extreme circumstances where, for example, a person has been murdered or has died in a terrorist attack, there might be strong and complicated feelings that you need professional help in dealing with.

Blame, however, can sometimes be misplaced. The need to hold someone accountable for a person's death can be a way of trying to make sense of something that is bewildering and seemingly random.

Blame can be directed at yourself as well as at others. The death was somehow *your* fault. You might feel guilty at your own sense of powerlessness. *I couldn't stop him from dying. I couldn't save her.* This sense of inadequacy is common in parents whose babies and children have died. They can feel as though they have failed to protect and nurture their children.

Self-blame is also a common legacy of suicide. When someone has ended their life deliberately, the sense of disempowerment for those left behind can be acute. *If only I'd listened more. If only I'd been a better parent. If only I'd realized how depressed she was.*

Blame might even be directed at the person who has died. A husband or wife might feel that their partner's death is a kind of abandonment. *How could she leave me on my own? Why did he go now?*

For people of faith, this anger might be directed at God. *Why didn't God look after my son as I prayed he would? Why did he make a world that has cancer in it? How could God let her suffer so much?*

Or anger might simply be directed at life, at the universe, at the precariousness of human existence. *It's so unfair! It's such a waste! It makes no sense!*

What people say

I experienced the most intense anger, bitterness and pain which raced through every part of me, and I shouted a host of expletives. My anger was directed not just at the evil creatures who had planted the bomb but at the injustice of Tim losing such a promising young life.
Colin Parry, writing about his twelve-year-old son Tim, killed by an IRA bomb

At funerals, the American Indians used to shoot spears and arrows into the sky, and at military funerals guns are still fired, in an apparent expression of fury.
Virginia Ironside

Feelings of anger can be tangled and messy. Perhaps you don't know *why* you're angry. Maybe you just feel irritable and grumpy. You find yourself snapping at your relatives or work colleagues. You seem to be on a short fuse all the time so that little things get out of proportion.

Maybe you found yourself lashing out at the florist or the undertaker on the day of the funeral, or felt furious with the vicar who took the service because she mispronounced your name.

Maybe you've lost your sense of humour and things get to you more – your coping mechanisms are less robust than they usually are.

It might be useful to try and identify what you really feel angry about. You could try writing a list that begins "I'm angry because…".

"I'm just *angry*!"

Maybe you have no idea why you are angry. You just *are*! So what do you do with those powerful and potentially destructive feelings?

The UK charity Winston's Wish gives bereaved children and their parents the opportunity, during weekend camps, to express anger by throwing things at a specially designated "Anger Wall". Having written down words or drawn pictures to identify the things they feel angry about, they pin these on the wall and throw lumps of wet clay at them. This exercise gives people permission to feel strong negative emotions and to let them out safely and without being judged or told to behave differently.

It might be that you would find a similar action helpful and cathartic. You could:

- throw something at a wall (choose something such as clay or potatoes that won't harm you or anyone else)
- hurl stones into a lake or river
- punch cushions
- go to a remote and preferably windy place (the top of a hill or a cliff-top path) and yell
- play squash, imagining that the ball is the thing or person you are angry with
- place an empty chair in a private room and imagine the person or thing you are angry with sitting in it – then say all the things you want to say but can't.

Mythbuster

I shouldn't feel angry. It's an inappropriate emotion. It must mean I'm a bad person.
Anger is a normal, healthy reaction to someone's death.
  Psychologist and bereavement expert Elisabeth Kübler-Ross wrote this:

… we live in a society that fears anger. People often tell us our anger is misplaced, inappropriate, or disproportionate. Some people may feel your anger is harsh or too much. It is their problem if they don't know how to deal with it… scream if you need to. Find a solitary place and let it out.

Your friends and relatives may find your anger difficult to handle. They may find you easier to "comfort" when you are sad than when you are bad-tempered and full of rage. Try to communicate how you are feeling if you can. If you have no one who will listen to you without telling you that you shouldn't be feeling like that, see a counsellor. It's OK to talk and to ask questions – even unanswerable ones. It's OK to be angry.

If you are dealing with a death as part of a bereaved family, don't be surprised if you find yourselves falling out with each other more than usual. Often, after a bereavement, dynamics and feelings which already existed seem to be amplified. If someone has had a lifelong sense of sibling jealousy or favouritism, these feelings of unfairness and resentment may flare after a parent's death. Tensions between family members may be made worse by money, property, a disputed will, or by a perception that the burdens have been unequally shared. For instance, a daughter who lived close to an ageing mother may feel angry that her brother who lived 200 miles away didn't share the responsibility for their mother's care. He in turn might feel guilty that he didn't arrive before she died. Bottling up these feelings might result in them having a blazing row about their mother's belongings that is about far more than is immediately apparent.

"I'll never forgive myself..."

Self-blame, regret, and guilt can be difficult to deal with. Perhaps you feel a bit stuck. There are things you wish you'd done or not done, decisions you made which you'd like to undo, things you said or never had the chance to say. It may sound like a cliché to talk of forgiving yourself, but you may find that, little by little, you are able to let go of a sense of blame and accept that you did your best. You were a "good enough" friend, son, daughter, parent, or spouse.

This self-forgiveness may be a long process, and using some kind of ritual might help you with it. Rituals allow you to mark significant changes, moments, or feelings by doing a physical action to symbolize something emotional or spiritual. Here are some you could try:

- Write things down and burn, bury or shred them.
- Drop pebbles into water to symbolize things you are sorry for.
- Build a cairn of stones to mark a change in your feelings.
- Prune or plant something.
- Tie knots in a rope and then untie them again.

9

Enjoying life again

In the last chapter we thought about guilt. It may be that you are feeling guilty because you are enjoying life again – or because you never stopped enjoying things in the first place. Someone you loved has died, but you still get pleasure from food or music or sex. You laugh at a programme on the television, you get caught up in banter in the office, you find yourself caring whether your football team wins or not – and then you feel bad because you've momentarily forgotten that you are bereaved and sad.

Survivor guilt
Perhaps you feel that because someone has died you have no right to enjoy life or that your pleasure somehow dishonours the dead. This is a bit like the

survivor guilt that people often feel when they have escaped death or injury in an incident in which others have died. *Why should I go on living when* they *can't?*

Perhaps your awareness that the person who has died is now unable to share the pleasure you are experiencing makes you feel uncomfortable and ambivalent. You make a snowman with your son and suddenly feel guilty at the realization that your brother who has died before having children will never have this experience.

What is "appropriate"?

The dissolving of any rules and etiquette around bereavement perhaps increases our anxiety about what is appropriate behaviour. In the past, laughter and entertainment might have been discouraged during the official observance of mourning. Certain activities might have been frowned upon or avoided. But now no such guidelines exist. So how do you know if it's all right to go on holiday or to the cinema? How do you know if it's OK to laugh or dance or go to the pub or fall in love? As with so much else, you are the best judge of what is right for you, so don't let other people impose their agenda on you or dictate what you do or don't do. You might not actually *feel* like going to a party or eating a sumptuous meal, but if you *do* feel like it, then why not do it?

In and out

It's completely normal to move in and out of grief and sadness, and in fact your system needs a rest, so anything you can do to give yourself a bit of "time out" will benefit you in the long term. Bereaved children especially need to be able to enjoy themselves and play. They may need to be given permission to do this and offered reassurance that it's all right if they don't feel sad all the time.

Mythbuster

I shouldn't laugh when I'm bereaved – it isn't respectful.

Laughter can be deeply therapeutic. It helps us release tension and is an important part of our coping mechanism. Dark "gallows" humour – laughing at life's absurdities – is common and natural for families managing a bereavement – all the more so if the person who has died was someone who laughed a lot or enjoyed a good joke!

Sometimes it helps to have a sense that your enjoyment is something the person who has died would have wanted. *She would have wanted me to go… He would have wanted me to be happy…* An awareness that the thing you are enjoying – the beautiful garden, the marvellous play, the thrilling sporting event – is something *they* would have loved can be bittersweet, both comforting and distressing at the same time. The very act of enjoyment reminds you of what you have lost, and your longing to share it with the person who has died underlines the pain of their absence. But your continued enjoyment of things is also an affirmation and celebration of life – yours and theirs. This is captured beautifully in the familiar, anonymous poem "Though I am dead":

Laugh and be glad
for all that life is giving,
and I, though dead,
will share your joy in living.

Doing things alone that you always did together can be very difficult, as can inhabiting places that were special to you both. The old Bing Crosby song "I'll be seeing you in all the old familiar places", which describes how places can be imprinted with the memories of someone now lost, is painfully true. Taking a trip back to a significant location may be very upsetting, so perhaps take someone along with you and allow yourself space and time to be sad. With any luck, it will be easier the second time you do it.

Feeling more alive

But what if you aren't feeling guilty at all? What if bereavement has actually increased your appetite for life? It might be that the death of someone significant has sharpened your appreciation of the things you enjoyed before. Now you're newly aware of your own mortality and of the fact that life can, and will, end, so you're more inclined to live in the present and enjoy things while you can. You find yourself noticing beauty more. You appreciate special moments with friends and family. You savour the tastes and smells of favourite foods. You throw yourself into everything with more abandon. Perhaps you even live dangerously for a time, craving that adrenaline rush, that thrill and intensity. This is normal too. You are asserting your aliveness, your defiance of death. A woman I knew whose husband died in his early sixties, within months of his retirement, talked poignantly about all the things they'd planned to do after he stopped work. "These days," she said, "I tell everyone, *Do it now*. Do things while you can."

Human beings are remarkably resilient, and the human spirit can find joy and delight even in the middle of tragic circumstances. Elisabeth Kübler-Ross writes movingly about seeing carvings of butterflies on the walls of a Nazi concentration camp: "As I walked through the huge barracks where people were housed in animal-like conditions, I noticed carvings on the walls... There was one image repeated over and over again – the image of butterflies... a symbol of transformation... of life continuing no matter what."

In the weeks, months, and years after a bereavement you will probably find yourself moving in and out of sadness and enjoyment, and at times experiencing several conflicting emotions simultaneously. You might find yourself laughing one minute and crying the next, but try not to let this worry you too much. As you begin to put your life back together, you will find that your ability to enjoy things starts to expand.

What people say

Actress Sheila Hancock writes of the death of her husband in her book *The Two of Us: My Life with John Thaw:*

Noticed it is a beautiful spring day. And I hate it because he can't see it. That's a waste. I have to learn to see the blossom. For myself, not just to tell John… I have always been in his shadow and never minded much when he was alive but now he's not here in person to cast the shadow and I need to get in the sun on my own.

A few months later she notices herself enjoying things again and writes:

I'm groping my way out of the dark. I accept every invitation I get and force myself out and about. Come on, girl, get your act together. This is it. Make the most of it before you too lose it. Life, I mean.

10

Resurfacing

Although people sometimes talk about *getting over* a bereavement, we established in Chapter 4 that this isn't a particularly helpful way of thinking. *Resurfacing* is perhaps a better image for the process of adjustment that follows someone's death – getting your head above water so that you are swimming rather than sinking. The water is still there, just as your loss is still there, but now you're managing better, you're not drowning.

Does it ever stop?
You might be wondering if you'll ever come to the end of grief, if you'll ever stop being bereaved. The reality is that grieving is often lifelong – it doesn't *end* as such – but there will, in all likelihood, be a gradual sense of lightening, of the pain easing, or of intense emotions

dimming a little. Some people describe this as a feeling of emerging from something, of coming out of a dark place into a brighter spot. You may find that, bit by bit, some of the symptoms we've explored – such as sleeplessness, desolation, disorganization, hopelessness, lack of energy, stress-related illness, anger, tearfulness – affect you less than they did. This doesn't mean that waves of raw grief won't knock you off balance from time to time, but you should notice a gradual improvement in your overall sense of well-being and your ability to cope with life.

In 1997 Australian psychologist Paul C. Burnett devised a means of measuring people's degree of recovery following a bereavement. His *Bereavement Phenomenology Scale* asks a series of questions such as "Do thoughts of X come into our mind whether you wish it or not?" (X being the person who has died), "When you dream about X does it feel as though X is still alive?" and "Do you find yourself pining for/ yearning for X?". Participants tick answers that range from "Always" or "Quite a bit of the time" to "A little bit of the time" and "Never". Psychologists use the numerical answers to discern whether a bereaved person feels they are making progress and beginning to feel better. There is, of course, no blueprint for exactly how this works, no template of "normal behaviour", and – as we've seen already – no fixed time frame for this progression from "Always" to "Never" – if, indeed, "Never" is ever reached.

Reinvestment in life

As the phenomena associated with bereavement gradually dominate your existence less than they once did, it's likely that you'll find yourself beginning to invest in life again. You may find yourself planning for the future and starting to look forward to things again. You might become more interested in other people and regain your appetite for life. If you have lost a partner, you may begin a new relationship or at least cease to feel that such a thing would be unimaginable. There is, of course, no "right time" to meet or marry a new partner. Some people start new relationships within a year or two years of a partner's death; others cannot even contemplate such an idea five or ten years further on. Those who meet or marry people sooner rather than later continue to grieve within the love and support of the new relationship, finding that loving a dead partner and loving a new partner aren't mutually exclusive.

If you find yourself in this situation, try not to let other people's reactions affect you too much. Outsiders are often quick to pass judgment on what they consider to be "decent" or "appropriate". Loving someone new doesn't mean you have forgotten the person who has died, just as having a new baby when a child has died doesn't mean you are trying to replace the dead child. You are simply reinvesting in life and rediscovering what it means for you to live positively. Be careful, though, and beware of making big decisions before you are ready to. (There is wise and frank advice about new relationships on the website **www.merrywidow.me.uk**.)

Getting over a bereavement is about letting go and moving on.

The phrases "letting go" and "moving on" are often used in relation to bereavement and recovery. Sometimes friends and relatives express impatience with the time bereavement takes, suggesting that the key to making "progress" is to forget the person who has died – to put the relationship behind you and make a fresh start.

In the 1980s, psychologist J. William Worden, a professor at Harvard Medical School, described bereavement in terms of four overlapping tasks, the final task being "To emotionally relocate the deceased and to move on with life". This "relocating" is about adjusting from a relationship with a living person to a relationship with a person who is no longer physically present, but it doesn't mean forgetting the person who has died or devaluing their significance.

Further research in 1996 from Klass, Silverman, and Nickman emphasized the "continuing bonds" with the deceased. Rather than "breaking bonds", they suggest that the process of grieving is about maintaining a bond with the person who has died that is compatible with new and continuing relationships.

Will I forget?

Perhaps you fear that as time passes, and as the "symptoms" of bereavement become milder, you will forget the person who has died. You will leave them further and further behind in the past, and their significance in your life will somehow diminish.

This is a common fear. Poet and artist Laurence Whistler, writing about the death of his wife, said, "A friend assured me… I should in time come through it… What was unendurable was precisely the idea of 'coming through'… Clarity was what I longed for now. If she faded altogether, I thought, that would be the real goodbye…"

All the while you feel the raw pain of loss, the person's memory seems sharp and intense. Maybe you fear that as you start to feel better, your recall of the person will become more hazy. How can you reinvest in life, start new relationships, and move forward, and yet still honour the importance of the person who has died and still acknowledge the magnitude of your love for them?

What people say

We don't want to get over it. The challenge is to ensure that we can accept Laurie's death into the narrative of our lives without destroying everything else we touch.
Sports writer Matthew Engel, whose teenage son died of cancer

I hope – I very much hope – that I will still in twenty or fifty years, however long I live… still get sudden

Will the pain get less?

If you have been quite recently bereaved, you may be wondering if you will ever feel better or if the pain will ever get less. As we said at the very start, you are unique and no one else's experience of bereavement will be identical to yours. There is, of course, no guarantee that you will gradually feel better, but it is very likely that you will. It might reassure you to read words of others who have experienced bereavement and found the pain slowly lifting. Jeremy Howe, whose wife Elizabeth was murdered at the age of thirty-four, wrote this:

Trust your instincts... Take each moment as it comes... And just put one foot forward at a time... you do get through it. And the advice I'd give to people – and it's terribly pat – is, it will get better. It doesn't mean you love that person any the less. It's just that time passes and you adjust to it.
Quoted in *Relative Grief*

And finally... remember:
- Pace yourself and go at your own speed.
- Express your feelings.
- Talk as much as you need to.
- Make sure you rest and eat properly.

- Don't make too many changes to your routine.
- Accept offers of help rather than struggling on alone.
- Don't be afraid to seek professional assistance if you feel you aren't making *any* progress or are somehow "stuck".

There's a list of organizations, websites, and books that may be helpful in the *Useful resources* section at the back of this book.

Above all, *do what feels right for you*. You are your own best guide.

For the family

Although bereavement is an individual and lonely process that has to be gone through by the bereaved person alone, you – their friends and relatives – can make a massive difference to how they feel and how well they cope along the way.

Remember, much as you may want to, you can't take away the pain that a bereaved person is experiencing or change the reality of their bereavement. But there is a lot that you *can* do…

Be practical

Practical help, especially in the first days and weeks after someone's death, can be of enormous value.

- Send cards and letters and include special memories and stories about the person who has died. Don't worry if you don't know what to say – just say *something*. Your words will probably be treasured for a long time afterwards.
- Offer specific help – ring and say, "I'm just off to the supermarket; can I get you something for tea?" Or

call and say, "Let me take your ironing so it's one less thing for you to think about." If you say something vague – "Let me know if there's anything I can do to help" – the chances are they *won't* ask, because they're not thinking clearly and can't make decisions, or because they feel awkward asking for help.

- Call on spec with flowers, food, or clean laundry – if you ring first, they might just say they're fine when they're not. But don't be offended if, when you call, it isn't a good moment. Assure them of your love and care, and say you'll come back at a better time. Ask them when a better time would be.

- Make or buy food and deliver it, unasked. It's likely that they won't have much of an appetite – or won't be thinking about looking after themselves – so things that can be left in the fridge and nibbled at are good. Journalist Emma Freud, writing in *The Guardian* newspaper after her father's death, said, "When someone dies, send a present – any present, but preferably cake."

- Keep them company. Offering to simply be with them or sleep in the spare room for a few days so they're not alone might help. Sometimes just the proximity of another person can be a comfort.

- Accompanying them when they have to do difficult tasks such as register the death, collect ashes from the undertaker, or sort out clothes and belongings can also be helpful.

Beyond the first few days and weeks there are many things you can continue to do:

- Marking significant anniversaries – the date when she was diagnosed with cancer, his birthday, the first Mother's Day since she died – with texts or cards or flowers can reassure someone that you are still thinking of them.
- Include widows or widowers in social groups or parties. Much of our socializing tends to be couples-based. Try to think of creative ways of including someone whose partner has died so that you decrease rather than increase their sense of isolation.
- Keep in touch – ring, call, arrange to go for a walk, a drink, or a coffee. Often bereaved people feel most alone several months after the person has died, when the first flurry of help and support has dissipated.

Aside from practical things, your friendship and the emotional support you give your bereaved friend or relative will be invaluable to them as they adjust to life without the person who has died. All relationships work differently, and you probably know best what your friends or family members need, but here are some do's and don'ts that might be useful.

Do's
- Do ask them what they most want and need, rather than assume you know already.

- Do encourage them to talk, but also respect their right not to.
- Do allow them to be honest.
- Do allow them to express sadness or anger without judging them or insisting that they "think positive".
- Do allow them to grieve in their own way and to go at their own pace.

Don'ts

- Don't avoid them because you don't know what to say or you fear upsetting them. Bereaved people often feel shunned by others. Meet them, make eye contact, start a conversation – even if it's difficult.
- Don't change the subject if they want to talk about the person who has died, about the details of their death, or about how they are feeling now. Let them tell you the same stories over and over again if necessary.
- Don't say "I know how you're feeling", because you probably don't. Even if you've experienced something similar, it won't feel exactly the same for them.

- Don't feel you have to have answers or solutions, or that you can make anything better, but be prepared to sit "empty-handed" and just listen – even if your instinct is to run away because it's too upsetting.
- Don't tell people how to behave or how they're "supposed" to be feeling. Remember that everyone is different.
- Don't take it personally if they are grumpy, abrupt, or irrational. The best friends of a bereaved person are the ones who have thick skins and robust egos. If you invite them to do something and they rebuff you and say they don't feel like it, ask them again another day. Don't take offence.
- Don't make tactless remarks. Don't tell a woman who has had a stillborn baby that she can always have another one. Don't tell a man whose wife has just died that he's bound to meet someone else. Don't tell people it was for the best. You may think you're helping by trying to make sense of something nonsensical, but if something just hurts, then it *just hurts*.

If you are supporting and helping a whole family through a bereavement, be aware that they may all be reacting differently and may have different – possibly conflicting – needs. Try to spend time with individuals separately so that they have space to grieve in their own way. For example, taking a bereaved child out for the day might give her opportunities to say things she can't say to her grieving parent or sisters. Or organizing childcare for a bereaved friend so that you can take him to the pub or go out for a walk may allow him to talk frankly without fear of upsetting his children. There may be groups or agencies in your neighbourhood that offer support to bereaved families or that host events which parents and children can attend, together or separately. Finding out about such events and networks and encouraging a friend to participate might be a way in which you can give real, practical help.

Get informed

Whatever your situation and whoever it is you are seeking to support, the more you understand about the process of bereavement the better. Reading the earlier chapters of this book will help you get an insight into what your friend or relative is going through. There are a number of other books listed in the *Useful resources* section which may deepen your understanding further. This section also lists a number of very helpful websites, online resources, and organizations.

Finally, remember that just by being there for your bereaved friend – by laughing and crying and sharing memories and muddling through – you are helping more than you could ever know.

Useful resources

Books you may find helpful

Rebecca Abrams, *When Parents Die: Learning to Live with the Loss of a Parent*, HarperCollins, 1999.

Neil Astley (Ed.), *Do Not Go Gentle: Poems for Funerals*, Bloodaxe Books, 2003.

Elizabeth Collick, *Through Grief: The Bereavement Journey*, Darton Longman and Todd/Cruse, 1986.

Jane Feinmann, *How to Have a Good Death: Preparing and Planning, with Informed Choices and Practical Advice*, Dorling Kindersley, 2006.

Tom Gordon, *New Journeys Now Begin: Learning on the Path of Grief and Loss*, Wild Goose, 2006.

Sheila Hancock, *The Two of Us: My Life with John Thaw*, Bloomsbury, 2004.

Virginia Ironside, *You'll Get Over It: The Rage of Bereavement*, Penguin Books, 1997.

Clare Jenkins and Judy Merry, *Relative Grief: Parents and Children, Sisters and Brothers, Husbands, Wives and Partners, Grandparents and Grandchildren Talk About Their Experience of Death and Grieving*, Jessica Kingsley, 2005.

Elisabeth Kübler-Ross, *On Death and Dying: What the Dying Have to Teach Doctors, Nurses, Clergy, and Their Own Families*, Collier Paperbacks (USA), 1970.

Elisabeth Kübler-Ross and David Kessler, *On Grief and Grieving: Finding the Meaning of Grief Through the Five Stages of Loss*, Simon and Schuster, 2005.

Tony Lake, *Living with Grief*, Sheldon Press, 1984.

C. S. Lewis, *A Grief Observed*, Faber and Faber, 1961.

Sue Mayfield, *Living with Bereavement: Practical, Emotional and Spiritual Help for Those Weathering Bereavement*, Lion Hudson, 2008.

Jane Morrell and Simon Smith, *We Need to Talk About the Funeral: 101 Practical Ways to Commemorate and Celebrate a Life*, Accent Press, 2007.

Blake Morrison, *And When Did You Last See Your Father?*, Granta, 1993.

Colin Murray Parkes, *Bereavement: Studies of Grief in Adult Life*, Pelican Books, 1975.

Colin and Wendy Parry, *Tim: An Ordinary Boy*, Hodder and Stoughton, 1994.

Janice Perkins, *How to Help a Child Cope with Grief: A Book for Adults Who Live and Work with Bereaved Children*, Foulsham, 2007.

Justine Picardie, *If the Spirit Moves You: Love and Life After Death*, Picador, 2001.

Ruth Picardie, *Before I Say Goodbye*, Penguin Books, 1998.

Lily Pincus, *Death and the Family: The Importance of Mourning*, Faber and Faber, 1976.

Suzanne Sjöqvist (Ed.), *Still Here With Me: Teenagers and Children on Losing a Parent*, Jessica Kingsley, 2006.

Susan Wallbank, *The Empty Bed: Bereavement and the Loss of Love*, Darton Longman and Todd, 1992.

Alison Wertheimer, *A Special Scar: The Experiences of People Bereaved by Suicide*, Routledge, 1991.

Laurence Whistler, *The Initials in the Heart*, Hart-Davis, 1964.

Wise Traveller: *Loss*, Scripture Union, 2007.

Books written for children

Debi Gliori, *No Matter What*, Bloomsbury, 2003.

Laurene Krasny Brown and Marc Brown, *When Dinosaurs Die: A Guide to Understanding Death*, Little, Brown and Company, 2004.

Michaelene Mundy, *Sad Isn't Bad: A Good Grief Guidebook for Kids Dealing with Loss*, University of Massachusetts Press, 2004.

Michael Rosen and Quentin Blake, *Michael Rosen's Sad Book*, Walker Books, 2004.

Doris Stickney, *Waterbugs and Dragonflies: Explaining Death to Young Children*, Geoffrey Chapman, 2004.

Susan Varley, *Badger's Parting Gifts*, Picture Lions, 1994.

Winston's Wish, *Muddles, Puddles and Sunshine: Your Activity Book to Help When Someone Has Died*, Hawthorn Press, 2007.

Useful resources

Organizations and websites

Agewell
www.agewell.org.nz
New Zealand based organization promoting the health of older people. Good web article "Loss and Change, Grief and Depression" about bereavement in old age (follow the link from "Sitemap").

Australian Centre for Grief and Bereavement
www.grief.org.au
Australian organization providing counselling, information, and clinical services to bereaved people. The "Resources" page contains a link to a huge range of international resources and support agencies.

Bereaved Parents of the USA
www.bereavedparentsusa.org
US-based self-help group for bereaved parents, grandparents, and siblings.

Citizen's Advice Bureau
www.adviceguide.org.uk
Helpful advice about practicalities and finance. Click on "Family" to select factsheets on "Wills", "What to do after a death", and "Dealing with the financial affairs of someone who has died".

The Compassionate Friends
www.compassionatefriends.org
International organization which supports families through the death of a child. Many local chapters worldwide and an online support community.

Counselling Directory
www.counselling-directory.org.uk/bereavement
Listing of UK counselling services, region by region.

Cruse Bereavement Care
www.crusebereavementcare.org.uk
Offers counselling and support to individuals, couples, and families living with bereavement.
PO Box 800
Richmond
Surrey TW9 1RG
Telephone: 020 8939 9530

RD4U
www.rd4u.org.uk
Cruse Bereavement Care's website for young people.

www.dying.about.com
Information site with section on "The Grieving Process" which includes "10 Tips to Help Yourself in Times of Grief".

The Dougy Center
www.dougy.org
Centre for support of bereaved children and families based in Oregon, USA. Excellent online resources and information for all ages.

FACTS Health Centre
Offers counselling, advice, and support when someone has died after being ill from AIDS.
FACTS Health Centre
126 Sheen Road
Richmond
Surrey TW9 1UR
Telephone: 020 8348 9195

The Foundation for the Study of Infant Deaths
www.fsid.org.uk
Cot death research and support.
11 Belgrave Road
London SW1V 1RB
Telephone: 020 7802 3200
Helpline: 080 8802 6868

GriefLink
www.grieflink.org.au
Australian information resource for bereaved people and their carers.

Helpguide
www.helpguide.org
American well-being information website with good article on "Grief and Loss".

If I Should Die
www.ifishoulddie.co.uk
Excellent, practical information about funerals, wills, and memorials.

International Stillbirth Alliance
www.stillbirthalliance.org
International organization supporting parents of stillborn children.

Khululeka
www.khululeka.org
South African grief support for children and young people.

Lifeline
www.lifeline.org.au
Australian website for support of those bereaved as a result
of suicide.

Merrywidow
www.merrywidow.me.uk
Highly readable and practical site, originally designed as a
survival guide for young widows, but now developed into an
online resource for anyone who has lost a partner.

The Miscarriage Association
www.miscarriageassociation.org.uk
The Miscarriage Association
c/o Clayton Hospital
Northgate
Wakefield
West Yorkshire WF1 3JS
Telephone: 01924 200799

The National Association of Widows
www.nawidows.org.uk
Organization run by the widowed for the widowed – men
and women.
48 Queens Road
Coventry CV1 3EH
Telephone: 0845 838 2261

New Zealand Government website
http://newzealand.govt.nz
Helpful information on "Bereavement and Wills" (type
"bereavement and wills" into the search bar).

Patient UK
www.patient.co.uk
Website with excellent section on "Benefits for Bereaved People"
(follow the link from "Benefits and Finance").

Road Peace
www.roadpeace.org
The UK's national charity for road crash victims provides support
to those bereaved or injured in a road crash.
Shakespeare Business Centre
245a Cold Harbour Lane
London SW9 8RR
Telephone: 020 7733 1603
Support line: 0845 4500 355

The Samaritans
www.samaritans.org.uk
Telephone UK: 08457 90 90 90
Republic of Ireland: 1850 60 90 90

Skylight – www.skylight.org.nz
New Zealand organization offering support and counselling to
children and young people dealing with change, loss, or grief.

The Stillbirth and Neonatal Death Society (SANDS)
www.uk-sands.org
28 Portland Place
London W1B 1LY
Helpline: 020 7436 5881

SANDS New Zealand branch
www.sands.org.nz

The War Widows Association of Great Britain
www.warwidowsassociation.org.uk
c/o 199 Borough High Street
London SE1 1AA
Telephone: 0845 2412 189

Winston's Wish – the Charity for Bereaved Children –
www.winstonswish.org.uk
4th Floor
St James's House
St James Square
Cheltenham
Gloucestershire GL50 3PR
Helpline: 08452 03 04 05
General enquiries: 01242 515157

Also currently available in the "First Steps" series:

First Steps out of Depression
Sue Atkinson

First Steps out of Eating Disorders
Dr Kate Middleton
and Jane Smith

First Steps out of Problem Drinking
John McMahon

First Steps out of Anxiety
Dr Kate Middleton

First Steps out of Problem Gambling
Lisa Ustok and Joanna Hughes

Printed in Great Britain
by Amazon